Poppy and the Play Date

Written by Krystal Grant

with the help of Madison, Collin and Chase Grant

ILLUSTRATED BY DARIN LORENZO HAGOOD

NOVELS BY KRYSTAL GRANT

Under the Palmetto Tree: A Novella

The Miseducation of Ms. G

Brooklyn

Poppy and the Playdate

Krystal Grant

F I R S T   E D I T I O N

ISBN: 978-1-942545-64-4

Library of Congress Control Number: 2016911141

Published by Kenely Books, An Imprint of Wyatt-MacKenzie

kenely@wyattmackenzie.com

For all the little children
who have passed through
the doors of my classroom
~ Krystal

For my family
~ Darin

Poppy loves wearing pink.

She has pink shoes.

She has pink shirts.

She has pink socks.

She has pink skirts.

Blake loves wearing blue.

He has blue shoes.

He has blue hats.

He has blue trucks.

He has blue bats.

Poppy decided that she would NEVER play with Blake because he does not wear the color pink.

One day Poppy went outside.

There was no one around . . .

except Blake.

Poppy watched Blake play.

He played in his sandbox.

He played on his slide.

He played on his bike.

He went for a ride.

Poppy was lonely.

Blake asked Poppy to play with him.

Poppy said, "YES!"

They played in the grass.

They played in the park.

They played on the swing.

They played until dark.

Poppy and Blake became friends.

And they played together every day.

The End

Author's Note

For three years I had the esteemed pleasure of working as a kindergarten teacher. It was a far cry from my many years teaching high school literature. Each day, my four and five year olds walked through my classroom door with bright eyes filled with wonder and excitement.

Our favorite part of the day was circle time. We would all sit *criss cross apple sauce* on my colorful carpet and immerse ourselves in stories told by amazing authors. Often times, I'd lose my voice because I read the stories with such volume and vigor. The students buckled over in laughter at my antics.

Being an educator is one of my greatest joys. I hope this book serves as a beacon of joy for your little one. Happy reading, my friends.

www.ingramcontent.com/pod-product-compliance
Lightning Source LLC
LaVergne TN
LVHW060643110826
845147LV00018B/1036

* 9 7 8 1 9 4 2 5 4 5 6 4 4 *